The Miracles of Francis Xavier

The Supernatural Ministry Of
Francis Xavier 1506 – 1552A.D.

IAN JOHNSON

The Miracles of Francis Xavier

Copyright © 2012
Ian Johnson

ISBN: 978-1-888081-92-3

Published by
Good News Ministries
220 Sleepy Creek Rd
Macon, GA 31210
800-300-9630

Dedication

To all seekers of Jesus in every generation and in every nation who take the mission to "go" and preach the Gospel seriously. And to the Teachers who inspire us to take up our cross and leave all that is comfortable, for the sake of the Gospel and for the Glory of Jesus Christ & His kingdom.

The Miracles of Francis Xavier

The Supernatural Ministry of Francis Xavier

CONTENTS:

The Mircales of Francis Xavier: Man on a Mission

This book is about the amazing life of Francis Xavier, missionary and pioneer to India, Sri Lanka, Malacca, Indonesia, the Islands of the Philippines and Japan. In the brief years between 1541 and his death in 1552 Francis saw thousands turn to Jesus; the miracles that followed his preaching of the gospel in these years are just like the book of Acts.

King John 3rd of Portugal was the sender who mostly financed Francis mission. Francis was the one who went and encouraged countless hundreds of others to do the same.

The aim of this book is to inspire your heart to missions, either as someone who goes, or as someone who sends. There are still millions who wait for the next Francis Xavier.

From a letter
By Francis Xavier to Simon Rodriguez ~ 1545

We are greatly indebted to the King of Portugal, our most excellent patron, and to the Portuguese who are in India, because of their great benevolence and liberality to us, we can hire many good labourers into Christ's vineyard so that the gospel can clearly be proclaimed and laid open to all that they might be saved.

ISAIAH 48:3

I have declared the former things from the beginning; they went forth from my mouth, and I caused them to hear it. Suddenly I did them, and they came to pass.

In declaring the miracles in the ministry of Francis Xavier, I pray that the Spark of his testimony will set a great fire in the lives of generations to come. We provide the sacrifice, He provides the fire and sparks a revival of the supernatural in the house of God.

HAGGAI 1:14

So the Lord sparked the enthusiasm of Zerubbabel governor of Judah, and the enthusiasm of Jeshua son of Zaddok, the high priest, and the enthusiasm of the whole remnant of God's people. They began to work on the house of their God, the Lord of Heaven's armies.

"Everyone should read this book to build their faith!"
**- Kathie Walters, international speaker/author
Good News Fellowship Ministries**

INTRODUCTION
BACKGROUND
&
EARLY LIFE

Apart from seeing the name on more than a few Church's and Schools I had never really heard of Francis Xavier. I didn't know that he was probably one of the most successful missionaries since the Apostle Paul, moving in the power of the book of Acts. But when I visited Goa in India in 2004 and again in 2005 I was confronted with the life of this Spiritual giant. While in Goa I discovered that not only had he made a huge impact on the west coast of India, but also in just about every region where the Portuguese had established a presence. In places such as India, Madagascar, Malacca, Ceylon, Indonesian and Japan, he saw thousands, perhaps millions touched and most often soundly saved and established in the faith.

As you will see later in this book, as he preached the Gospel, signs wonders and amazing miracles followed the preaching of Jesus. All this was in a window of just 11 years from 1541-1552. As we travel through the pages of this supernatural journey we can once again hear Francis Xavier's challenge to missions both in the area of helping the poor and in the totally abandoned life that saw the miraculous as an every day occurrence.

We will also be challenged to support such supernatural endeavours even as the King of Portugal supported Francis, because as it was then, so it is now. Some are called to go, and some are called to send. The aim of this book is to stimulate a passion for the mission of preaching the Kingdom of God with signs following, to stir the pocket book of the senders, and release the passion of those who are to go. There are billions of souls in the world who have never heard the gospel. Perhaps you are the next Francis Xavier.

Francis would today be called an extremist. He so desired to be martyred for Christ that it caused him to be fearless in his expression of faith. He didn't die a martyr, he succumbed to a fever. Never the less, he left a legacy of salvation in the East that others are today building upon.

Thankfully for us, Francis was a prolific letter writer, and many of these letters have been preserved in Portugal and in India. This has given us a clear picture and record of the passion, humility and anointing that was on his life.

Over the 500 years since the birth of Francis, much has been written about him, mostly by Catholic writers and most, far more educated than I am. This book is not an attempt to negate any of these writings but rather an attempt to put into modern language the supernatural Ministry of Francis Xavier.

Francis Xavier was born in Navarre at the castle of Xavier near Pamplona in 1506. His mother was heiress of the two illustrious houses; Azpilcueta and Xavier and his father, Don John de Jasso, was one of the chief counsellors of state to John III d'Albert the king of Navarre. Among their numerous family of children, Francis was the youngest; those that were elder bore the surname of Azpilcueta, the younger, that of Xavier.

Although not a lot has be written or recorded of his early life, that which has been leads us to suggest he was of a complying nature with a keen sense of humour and a great aptitude for learning to which he gave himself. While all his brothers embraced the profession of soldiers in the army of the King of Navarre, his inclination toward learning caused his parents to send him to Paris at the age of eighteen where he entered the college of St. Barbara to study scholastic philosophy.

After two years he graduated with a Master of Arts. He then taught philosophy at Beauvais College, though he continued to live at St. Barbara. Very soon Francis' life was about to change forever.

BACKGROUND TO
THE CALL

THE INFLUENCE OF
IGNATIUS LOYOLA

Background to the Call

In studying the life of Francis Xavier it seems clear, that in Paris or on his travels around Europe he had no real immediate plans of going to the Portuguese East Indies. One thing is certain however, Francis was totally abandoned to Jesus.

In Paris it is recorded that Francis was equally at home fellowshipping with true believers either Catholic or Lutheran; to him Christ was all.

Francis went to India and the East by the hand of God. If it were not for the inclement health of a man named Bobadilla, the one originally called to go to Goa in India on behalf of the King of Portugal, we may not have seen the true Francis come forth. But because he was abandoned to God's purpose, he went wherever the Lord willed.

As I ask around Evangelical or Pentecostal circles, there is very little knowledge of the Acts of Francis Xavier in the East, which is a shame because to Francis it was all about Jesus. The Catholic Church was the only missionary sending vehicle at the time, so Francis became a famous Catholic saint. In the 500 years since the protestant Church has largely ignored him.

If Francis were to speak on Earth today he would implore you to devotion and an abandoned heart and life to Jesus. Jesus was his master and

Lord who he loved so dearly and gave up his whole life in the service of. He would call you to preach the gospel not counting the cost. Francis Xavier was a man who travelled roughly 38,000 miles by sea and land during 11 years of his missionary work. If he had stayed in the courts of the King of Portugal, he may well have lived a lot longer life. But the question I have to ask is, who now knows the names of the men who served in the royal courts in 1552? This man inspires me. I hope he inspires you in these pages also.

The impact of Ignatius Loyola

Any history of Francis Xavier cannot be completed without recognising the impact that Ignatius Loyola had upon the young man in Paris. Ignatius had become a Christian at the age of 30. and was the youngest of thirteen children. At the age of sixteen he was sent to serve as a page to Juan Velazquez, the treasurer of the kingdom of Castile.

As a member of the Velazquez household, he was frequently at court and developed a taste for all it presented, especially the ladies. He was much addicted to gambling, very contentious, and not above engaging in swordplay on occasion. For a number of years he went about in the dress of a fighting man, wearing a coat of mail and breastplate, and carrying a sword and other sorts of arms. Eventually in May of 1521, at the age of 30, he found himself serving as an officer at Pamplona against the French, who had claimed the territory as their own against Spain. The Spaniards were terribly outnumbered and the commander of the Spanish forces wanted to surrender, but Ignatius convinced him to fight on for the honour of Spain if not for victory.

During the battle a cannon ball struck Ignatius, wounding one leg and breaking the other. Because they admired his courage, the French soldiers carried him back to recuperate at his home, the castle of Loyola rather than to prison. During the long weeks of his recuperation, he was extremely bored and asked for some romance novels to pass the time. Luckily there were none in the castle of Loyola, but there was a copy of the life of Christ and a book on the Fathers of the early Church.

Desperate, Ignatius began to read them. The more he read, the more he considered the exploits of Jesus and his followers worth imitating. This experience was the beginning of his conversion, and his early notes the beginning of his work, "Spiritual Exercises". The *Exercises* recognize that not only the intellect but also the emotions and feelings can help us to come to knowledge of the action of the Spirit in our lives.

Eventually, completely converted from his old desires and plans of romance and worldly conquests, and recovered from his wounds enough to travel, he left the castle in March of 1522. He continued towards Barcelona but stopped along the river Cardoner at a town called Manresa. He stayed in a cave outside the town, intending to linger only a few days, but he remained for ten months and had multiple daily encounters with the Lord and visions of heaven and hell. The cave became his vehicle into the mystical realms of Christ and His Kingdom.

He spent hours each day in prayer and also worked in a hospice. It was while here that the ideas for what are now known as the *Spiritual Exercises* began to take shape in the form of a book.

It was also on the banks of this river that he had visions which are regarded as the most significant in his life. The visions were   an enlightenment about which he later said that he learned more on one occasion than he did in the rest of his life. Ignatius never revealed exactly what the visions were about, but they seem to have been encounter's with God as He really is in heaven. The result for Ignatius was that he saw all creation in a new light and acquired new meaning and relevance and experience that enabled Ignatius to find God in all things.

Ignatius now 33 years old, was determined to study for the priesthood. However, he was ignorant of Latin, a necessary preliminary to university studies in those days. So he started back to school studying Latin grammar in a school in Barcelona. After two years he moved on to the University of Alcala. There his zeal got him in trouble, a problem that continued throughout his life. He would gather students and adults to explain the Gospels to them and teach them how to pray. His efforts attracted the attention of the Inquisition and he was once thrown into jail for 42 days.

When he was released he was told to avoid teaching others. Because he could not live without helping souls, Ignatius moved on to the University of Salamanca. There, within two weeks, the Dominicans had thrown him back into prison again. Though they could find no heresy in what he taught. Once more he took to the road, this time for Paris.

At the University of Paris he began school again, studying Latin grammar and literature, philosophy, and theology. It was also in Paris that he began sharing a room with Francis Xavier and Peter LeFevre. He greatly influenced Xavier and LeFevre directing them at one time or another in what we now call the *Spiritual Exercises*. LeFevre , who was not taken up with the world, resigned himself without opposition.

But Francis, whose head was full of ambitious thoughts, made a long and vigorous resistance, and rallied Ignatius on all occasions, ridiculing the meanness and poverty in which he lived as a degenerate lowness of soul. Ignatius repaid his contempt with meekness and kindness, and continued to repeat sometimes to him, "What will it profit a man to gain the whole world, and lose his own soul?"

By 1535, Francis Xavier performed Ignatius's spiritual exercises with such fervour that he passed four days without taking any nourishment and his mind was taken up day and night in the contemplation of heavenly things. By these meditations, which sank deep into his soul, he was wholly changed into another man, in his desires, affections, and views.

Afterwards he did not know himself and the humility of the cross appeared to him more desirable than all the glories of this world. In the most profound sentiments of compunction he made a personal confession of faith in Jesus Christ, and from that point formed a design of glorifying God by all possible means and of employing his whole life for the salvation of souls.

Soon the three friends had become nine and nine companions departed from Paris on the 15th of November, 1536, to go to Venice. Their plan was to go on to the Holy Land. They arrived at Venice on the 8th of January, 1537. Ignatius, directed they divide themselves to serve the poor in two hospitals in that city. In 1538 the companions had moved to Rome. In Rome they were introduced to Govea, a Portuguese, formerly president of the college of St. Barbara, at Paris. John III, King of Portugal, had sent him on some important business.

He had formerly known Ignatius & Xavier, at Paris, and had been a great admirer of their virtue; and he became more so at Rome, insomuch that he wrote to his master the King that men so learned, humble, & inflamed with zeal, untiring in labour, lovers of Jesus Christ, and who aimed at nothing but the honour of God, were fit to be sent to plant the faith in the East Indies.

The king wrote thereupon to Don Pedro Mascaregnas, his ambassador at Rome, and ordered him to obtain six of these apostolic men for this mission. Ignatius could grant him only two, and selected Simon Rodriguez, a Portuguese, and Nicholas Bobadilla, a Spaniard. The former went immediately by sea to Lisbon; Bobadilla, who waited to accompany the ambassador, fell sick, and by an overruling supernatural direction, Francis Xavier was substituted on the day before the ambassador began his journey.

Xavier left Rome with the ambassador on the 15th of March, 1540, The entire journey was performed by land over the Alps and Pyrenees, and took more than three months. At Pampelona, the ambassador pressed the Francis to go to the castle of Xavier, which was but a little distant from the road, to visit his mother who was still living, and his other friends, whom he would probably never see in this world again.

But Francis would not turn aside to see his loved ones, saying that he deferred the sight of his relations till he should visit them in heaven; that this transient view would be accompanied with melancholy and sadness, the products of last farewells, whereas their meeting in heaven would be for eternity and without any sorrow. This wonderful disengagement from the world affected Mascaregans so profoundly that he was converted to a new course of life in Christ.

They arrived at Lisbon about the end of June, and Francis went immediately to Rodriguez, who was lodged in a hospital, in order to attend and instruct the sick. They made this place their abode they were retained by the king at Lisbon, and Francis was obliged to stay there eight months, while the fleet was getting ready to sail in spring. Dr. Martin d' Azpilcueta, commonly called the Doctor of Navarre, an uncle to Xavier by his mother's side, was then chief professor of divinity at Coimbra, and wrote several letters to Francis offering various posts in the Kings court. But could not engage him; Francis had abandoned himself to the purpose of God in the East.

It was on the 7th April 1541 in the 36th year of his life that Francis Xavier finally set sail on board the admirals vessel. The ship also carried Don Martin Alfonso de Sousa, General-Governor designate to the Indies who had been given five ships to take possession of his government. The admiral's vessel's contained at least a thousand persons, whom Francis considered as committed to his care.

He preached every Sunday before the main-mast, took care of the sick, converted his cabin into an infirmary, lay on the deck, and lived on charity during the whole voyage. Francis landed at Goa in India on the 6th of May, in 1542, in the thirteenth month from their setting out from Lisbon. Thus the missionary adventures of Francis Xavier were about to begin in earnest.

There are many miracles recorded prior to Francis Xavier arriving in India. And some of these will be covered in the chapter Miracles Signs and wonders later in the book.

Francis was a model for missionaries, formed upon the spirit of the apostles and in all events was perfectly resigned to the will of God, from where it seems proceeded a tranquillity of soul, a perpetual cheerfulness, and equality of countenance.

*He rejoiced in afflictions and sufferings and said that "one, who had once experienced the sweetness of suffering for Christ, will ever after find it worse than death to live without a cross." By humility, Francis Xavier was always ready to follow the advice of others and attributed all blessings to their prayers in the many letters he wrote. (4)

Such a heart and mind cannot be emulated by zeal that comes from man's own striving but is a result of a life surrendered through encounters with the living, indwelling Christ.

(4) From Henry James Coleridge "The life and letters of Francis Xavier" Burns & Oats publisher London. (1874)*

THE GLORY OF
THE MISSION
AND
THE ABANDONED HEART

The mission of Francis Xavier was effective in reaching the un-reached, because it came with demonstrations of God's Glory. Francis would be the first to say that the supernatural gifts he moved in were not from him, but from the Master whom he loved and abandoned his life to.

The supernatural manifestations of the Holy Spirit are the foundation stones upon which the church was established and upon which it stands.

The miracles in Francis Xavier's life came out of relationship with Jesus and abandoned obedience to the purpose of God. When I questioned the Lord recently I said, "Lord you seemed to do anything Francis asked you to do", the Lord replied, "Because Francis did anything I asked him to do."

There are many stories of the devotional life of Francis Xavier. It all began with the "Spiritual exercises of Ignatius Loyola" but as time went by Francis would love nothing better than to be shut away in a room or in the grand gardens of Goa with no one but Jesus. On the occasions that people were able to spy through the window or see through the cracks in a wall, Francis was observed in what the Catholic Church calls Ecstasy of spirit. Often in these times alone with the Lord he would be caught up in visions or transported into heaven. He received all his instructions in this way.

Francis emulated his master, in only doing what he heard the Father saying. This type of devotion is costly, but those who practise it, abandon themselves to it regardless of the cost. Even in his preaching he would always give way to the moving of the Holy Spirit or the voice of the Father. One such recorded event happened in October 1549 while Francis Xavier was in Malacca. The Archinese navy had attacked Malacca, and then challenged the Portuguese to a naval battle. Francis sought the Lord and got word from him that they should go up against them.

For weeks it seemed as if the whole Portuguese fleet was lost, as no word came back. Most of the fighting men were regular soldiers with wives and children. Belief in the worst having happened began to grow in Malacca, chiefly among the members of the families of the soldiers. To create panic, the news was circulated that the Portuguese had been defeated and massacred. Wives, mothers, sisters and relatives began to mourn for the lost relatives. The whole blame was thrown on Francis.

On Sunday, the 4th December 1549, a good crowd of people were attending service on St. Paul's Hill. Xavier went up to the pulpit to preach. In the course of his sermon, he suddenly became silent, like one carried out of himself and beholding events at a distance. His hands were tightly compressed; his eyes were immovably fixed on the cross suspended from the vault of the church, his countenance varying, expressing joy at times and grief at others. He was heard uttering incoherent sentences, half completed words, as is usual in cases of ecstasy but, soon it became evident to his audience that he was watching some feat of arm.

Suddenly he became completely serene, as if things had happened as he had wished. His arms and head fell on the pulpit. He remained in that attitude, in complete silence for thirty minutes. Everyone present was silent, breathless with anxiety and surprise. The Church was filled with the fear of the Lord. The suspense was short lived. For Xavier, raising his head, his face glowing like that of an angel, emphatically exclaimed, "Brethren, let us all together be in thanksgiving to God for the victory of our fleet. The Achinese have been defeated.

On Friday, the news will reach us and soon afterwards the victorious fleet with its men will be with us." Having said this he left the pulpit. Upon hearing this announcement, the people of Malacca who had been terribly depressed by listening to false reports, burst into joy. On Friday, some people flocked to the shore while others went to St. Paul's hill to watch the approach of some distant sail. They were not disappointed for on that day, Manuel Godinho reached the Malacca harbour, commissioned to bring the news of victory to D. Francisco de Mello the Governor. Soon after the fleet arrived, the Governor with the whole city welcomed the fighting men with great joy. Francis, most radiant, thanked and embraced them.

The soldiers then reported that at the most crucial moment of the battle; they saw the man of God encouraging them on the lead vessel. A miracle of bi-location written into the annuls of Portuguese history.

A man abandoned in Love for Jesus

Francis took Jesus at his word, which was, if he should go away it would be better than ever for his people, for God would walk with them more than in all the ages past. His promise was;

"It is expedient for you that I go away, for if I do not go away the comforter will not come unto you; but if I go, I will send him to you." John16:7

"He that believes in me the works that I do shall he do also". John 14:12.

Jesus has gone to the Father in Heaven and the Holy Spirit has come to take his place; to carry on his uncompleted task, to work in the midst of His church in signs and wonders and gifts of the Holy Spirit. The trances, visions, revelations, miracles and supernatural manifestations seen in the Life of Francis Xavier are meant to be the normal experiences of every believer in the supernaturally founded, supernaturally filled, and supernaturally directed church of Jesus Christ.`

The important thing to remember is that even in the midst of all these miracles, and wonders, Francis still suffered from the frailty of being human. To anyone who reads between the lines of the story of his life the fact of his humanness is evident.

This should encourage us that even in our frailty God will use us to change the world. In his own day, and among some of his peers, he was by no means the great success we, looking back, can see him to have been. On the contrary, we are not without proofs, both internal and external, that to many at least of his contemporaries he was thought a failure.

He had staunch friends who knew him well, and his capacity for friendship is manifest in every letter that he wrote, still there is, throughout his life, a certain isolation and loneliness which cannot be mistaken. At times he seems almost to cry out against it; when, for instance, he writes to all his brethren in Europe, saying he would gladly write to each one if he could; when in his moments of distress he addresses a single faithful follower in India; then he leaves all alone and hides himself away to seek the one Friend who, he knows, would never fail him. Jesus was his only true companion in the East and to him he clung relentlessly.

In his letters we have evidence of his own deep conviction that he felt he was of little worth. By nature highly strung and sanguine, he suffered from strong reactions; endowed with talents and gifts beyond the ordinary, he was weighed down with the littleness of men around him, blocking his way at every turn; a man of broad horizons and boundless ambitions, he seemed forever tempted to depression and despair, and to surrender every task he undertook.

The real greatness of the man must surely lie in this, that he did what he did in spite of ever discouragement from without and from within. If Jesus gave him an instruction he carried it out with passion and zeal despite his circumstances.

This zeal and passion led him in an ecstasy of love for his Jesus. It seems at times his heart would burst with the joy of knowing him. As he filled his soul again and again in these times of set apartness, the stage was set for the next season of miracles, preaching to the lost and serving the poor and sick wherever he found himself.

His life it seems was perpetually marked by three foundational tenants of Christianity. Evangelism, demonstrations of supernatural power and servant hood to the poor and suffering.

MIRACLES SIGNS
&
WONDERS

Miracles in the ministry of Francis Xavier are a big part of his success in reaching the lost. To list them all would require many pages. I have listed six instances of the Lord raising the dead through the ministry of Francis Xavier. It is recorded that there were more than Twenty eight and most probably many more than that.

Francis himself never wrote or boasted about his ministry, he was always more concerned about the welfare of others. But upon his death the King of Portugal asked that testimonies be gathered concerning this ministry.

Many who had witnessed the glory of God demonstrated in these ten years had themselves perished before such testimony could be gathered. But those who were still around and able, freely testified about this remarkable servant of Christ.

Some of the recorded miracles
(4)* From Henry James Coleridge "The life and letters of Francis Xavier" Burns & Oats publisher London. (1874)

Raised a drowned boy

He was about to conduct a service at Combutur, when a crowd entered with the corpse of a boy who had drowned in a well. The mother threw herself at the feet of Francis and implored him to restore the life of the Child. After a short prayer Francis took the boy by the hand and bade him arise. The child rose up at once, and ran to his mother.

Raised a youth bitten by a Cobra

A youth who had been baptised by Francis was in the night bitten by a Cobra and was found in the morning dead. Francis touched the foot with Silvia from his mouth, made the sign of the cross, took him by the hand and bade him rise as if he had been simply asleep. It should also be noted here that one of these Children who Francis instructed in preaching the Gospel also is credited with raising two people from the dead.

Raised a man buried and putrefying

Francis Xavier was preaching one day at Coulon, a village in Travancore near Cape Comorin, perceiving that none were converted by his discourse; he made a short prayer that God would honour the blood and name of his beloved Son by softening the hearts of the most obdurate. Then he bade some of the people open the grave of a man who was buried the day before, near the place where he preached; and the body was beginning to putrefy with a noisome scent, which he desired the bystanders to observe. Then falling on his knees, after a short prayer, he commanded the dead man in the name of the living God to arise. At these words the dead man arose and appeared not only living but vigorous and in perfect health.

Disrupted a funeral

The Lord also raised to life through Francis, on the same coast, a young man who was a Christian, whose corpse he met as it was being carried to the grave. To preserve the memory of this wonderful action the parents of the deceased, who were present, erected a great cross on the place where the miracle was wrought. These miracles made so great impressions on the people, that the whole kingdom of Travancore was subjected to Christ in a few months, except the king and some of his courtiers.

Raises a Girl three days dead and in a tomb

Bartoli gives the following account that occurred in Malacca January 1546.
There was a very conspicuous miracle, the recalling to life of a girl who had been three days buried. She was the daughter of a recent convert, and had died when Francis was out of town. The Mother had sought Francis every where when her child became ill, but she died long before his return.

As soon as the woman heard of his return, she took courage to think that he might be able to raise her from the dead. So she went at once to him, and throwing herself at his feet in floods of tears, began to say to him, exactly as Martha did to Jesus, If you had been here my daughter would have lived.

So come now and ask the Lord to bring life back into her. Francis marvelled to see her faith, seeing as how she had not long been a believer. He lifted his eyes to heaven and prayed God to grant her consolation; then he turned to the woman and said resolutely that she was to go, that her daughter was alive.

She between hope and fear, did not disbelieve his word, but because he had not offered to come with her to the place where the dead girl was, to raise her to life, she answered that she had been buried three days. "It matters not" said Francis "go and open the grave and you will find her alive". The woman made no more questions but with great faith and rejoicing ran to the church, and there in the sight of many others, caused the stone to be raised off the grave and found the child alive.

Raises daughter of Japanese nobleman ~ snatches her from Hell

Here is another witness from beyond the grave. History avers that when St. Francis Xavier was at Cangoxima, in Japan, he performed a great number of miracles, of which the most celebrated was the resurrection of a maiden of noble birth.

This young damsel died in the flower of her age, and her father, who loved her dearly, believed he would become crazy. Being an idolater, he had no resources in his affliction, and his friends, who came to console him, rendered his grief only the more poignant.

Two newly converted Christians who came to see him before the funeral of her whom he mourned day and night, advised him to seek help from Francis who was doing such great things, and demand from him with confidence, the life of his daughter.

The pagan - persuaded by the young Christians that nothing was impossible to the (holy man), and beginning to hope against all human appearances, as is usual with the afflicted, who readily believe whatever comforts them - went to Francis Xavier, fell at his feet, and with tears in his eyes, entreated him to bring to life again his only daughter whom he had just lost, adding that it would be to give life to himself.

Xavier, touched by the faith and sorrow of the pagan, went aside with his companion, Fernando, to pray to God. Having come back again after a short time, he said to the afflicted Father, *"Go, your daughter is alive!"* The idolater, who expected that Francis would come with him to his house and invoke the name of the God of the Christians over his daughter's body, took this speech as a jest and withdrew, dissatisfied.

But scarcely had he gone a few steps when he saw one of his servants, who, all beside himself with joy, shouted from a distance that his daughter was alive. Presently, he beheld her approaching. After the first embraces the daughter related to her father that, as soon as she had expired, two horrible demons pounced upon her and sought to hurl her into a fiery abyss, but that two men, of a venerable and modest appearance, snatched her from the hands of these executioners and restored her life, she being unable to tell how it happened.

The Japanese understood who these two men of whom his daughter spoke were, and he led her directly to Xavier to return him such thanks as so great a favour deserved. She no sooner saw Francis with his companion, Fernando, than she exclaimed: *"There are my two deliverers!"* And at the same time, the daughter and the father yielded to Jesus and demanded Baptism.

Woman saved in Childbirth

One day as Francis passed through a village of the Paravas in South Indian where no one was willing to become Christian because of the chief of the area had forbidden it. There was there however a woman who had been in labour three days. She was weak and near death.

Francis called on the Lord proclaiming that "The earth is the Lords and the fullness thereof and all who dwell in it" Francis explained to her the truth of salvation through Jesus, and asked her if she wanted to receive this truth. She did and gladly.

Francis baptised her and immediately she gave birth. The whole village was soon full of the news that a miracle had taken place. But still not wanting to offend their chief said they could not become Christian. Francis asked to be taken to this ruler, and immediately proclaimed to him the good news of the gospel, as Francis spoke he was lifted off the ground and a supernatural glow appeared around him.

The chief responded by calling on the name of the Lord in fear. Very soon the whole area was hearing about the miracle of birth and supernatural reinforcement of the Gospel. It is said that as a result of this miracle over 10,000 souls came to Jesus in one month.

Francis writes to Ignatius describing the healing of the sick

To Master Ignatius Loyola from Francis Xavier sent from Cochin Dec 31st 1543.

I and Francis Mancias are now living among the new Christians at Comorin. They are very numerous and are increasing every day. The fruit that is being reaped here I trust heartily. By the grace of God they show an ardent love for Jesus and an extraordinary zeal for learning and imparting it to others.

Every day a vast number of sick natives come to us for prayer, there are too many to pray for each day, so I have taught the Children to pray and a great number of sick persons are restored daily to health by way of their prayers, I have also taught these Children to teach the rudiments of the Christian Gospel, sharing it with those who are healed, and so daily the message of Jesus is spread through out the villages.

Jesus has made the very disease of their bodies the occasion of calling upon his name and into salvation. The Holy Spirit is drawing them into faith almost by force. There remains therefore only one reason for men not becoming Christians, and that is that there are not enough labourers to tell them.

Gift of Tongues

Many testimonies and much evidence is found in letters from this time that Francis Xavier possessed the gift of Tongues. The evidence witnesses to him having the power of clearly and freely speaking in the Dialects of the numerous different tribes among whom he preached. In India, the Moluccas (Indonesian) and Japan.

Altogether it is supposed that he must have had to preach to as many as thirty different nations, with dialects of their own, as separate nations. It is particularly stated in the evidence that his possession of this gift was notorious, and was considered by the natives themselves as a mark of his mission from God. The occasions on which this took place were when he preached to vast crowds.

In January 1546 Francis sailed from Malacca on a vessel with a crew made up of many different heathens in race and language. The voyage lasted six weeks and Francis preached with great zeal instructing these wild mariners in the ways of the Lord. The evidence of the process proves that Francis was empowered with the gift of tongues.

*Note – there is a difference to Speaking in tongues for our edification through he baptism of the Holy Spirit (which Francis also possessed) and the Gift of tongues which is when someone speaks and all understand regardless of their language.

Because men of different language understood him all at the same time, each in their own dialect. And this made the men much more docile toward the preaching of the word

.

Leper healed.

A begger covered with sores and putrid wounds asked alms of him, and Francis washed him with his own hands, drank the water and sent him on his way totally healed.

Bi-location miracles.

Francis Xavier is reported to have been at several places at the same time preaching to the natives. So carefully witnessed were these bi-locations and so numerous were they that Pere Bouhours biographer admits that the "bi-locations which are related in the story of St. Francis Xavier would seem to be of quite ordinary occurrence."

The fact I am now about to record is to be found in the "Vie de Saint Francois Xavier," by Pere Bouhours (Avignon, 1817, Vol. II). Let me introduce this wonderful example of bi-location by a statement made by the author in his preface to this very readable volume. He writes: "No miracles were ever examined with greater care, or were subjected to a more crucial test, than those presented for the canonization of Francis Xavier."

Early in November, 1551, the ship on which Francis Xavier the missionary was sailing from Japan to India entered the Straits of Korea. Early one morning the vessel rode into one of those fierce and prolonged storms which carry fear to the hearts of seasoned mariners.

A hurricane swept the decks, carried away the sails, tore out the masts, and threatened destruction to the ship and all on board. Then Francis fell upon his knees in prayer, when presently the sea went down and the ship, water-logged, floated helplessly. The crew got out the boat and began to tow the ship to the nearest land. While they were rowing the storm again rose, the tow-line was snapped and the oarsmen and their boat swept out to sea. The tempest grew to a tornado, when the Francis retired to his room invoking the Holy Name, besought Jesus Christ by the five wounds inflicted on Him when nailed to the cross to save them.

As he prayed, the storm passed beyond them. The sailors on the ship were now overwhelmed with sorrow for the fate of their companions driven out to sea. Then Francis said to them: "Be of good cheer, my friends, for before the expiration of the third day the daughter that is lost will return to her mother." Their water-logged wreck rose and sank with the waves, and yet no boat returned.

In vain they scanned the horizon and saw no sign of a boat. They were giving up all hope, when again Francis cheered their drooping spirits: "Have courage, my children," he pleaded, "I tell you they are returning to us." Then he retired to his berth and, once again, fell upon his knees in prayer. Presently the "lookout" shouted, "They are coming," and every eye took in the rowing men.

A cry of joy greeted the saved men, who, reaching the side of the ship mounted and were embraced by their companions. When the hand-shakings and congratulations were over, the quartermaster gave orders to have the returned boat brought on deck. "Wait, wait," cried one of the rescued men, "Father Francis, where is he? He has not come aboard." The sailors who remained on the ship, hearing the man and his companions thus express themselves, said one to the other: "The poor fellows are out of their minds from long suffering and starvation." But in vain they tried to disabuse the minds of the returned men by pointing to the empty boat, and by assuring them that Father Francis was now on board and had, at no time, left the ship.

To the amazement of every one the saved men persisted in asserting that from morning till night and from night till morning, Francis was with them for three days. "No, No," they exclaimed, "we had no fear of being lost or of perishing, for the holy man was with us and told us we would be saved." "Many of the witnesses say that Xavier appeared to those who were in the boat tossed about by the waves, and that when they were taken up into the ship Xavier had been all the time with them in the boat, and that they were filled with astonishment when they found that at the same time he had been on the ship."

Francis Xavier Marches against an Army

The Vadhouger or Badages were determined to rule the Comorin coast and were conducting raids against the Christians. The Historian Bartoli gave the following account of an event that occurred near the city of Cotate. A Church still exists on the plain a few miles north of Cotate commemorating this heroic action by Francs Xavier.

It would appear that the invasion of Travancore was made by a formidable army who then turned their attention to the fishery coast. The particular attention of this attack appears to be the villages of the new Christians and when Francis heard of the imminent attack he marched toward the oncoming army holding a cross, and he rebuked them in the name of Jesus.

The front ranks stopped and urged those behind to turn around. Because standing in front of them they saw a man of great height, of terrible and majestic appearance in a black robe, overawed and frightened, they could not bear the fire that flashed from his face and eyes. The leaders fell to the ground by some unknown power, and the rest of the army turned and fled. More than a dozen witnesses came forward to testify in writing all recounting the same story.

Sweet water from the Sea

This miracle is one of those which were specially selected from the Processes by the auditors of the Rota as being beyond all doubt and cavil. The eye-witnesses, whose names are given, and who swore to the truth of these facts at Cochin, are two whose names occur in the letters of St. Francis at this time : Domenico Caldeira, who was 98 years old when he was examined and Joam Botello, who was 85. Botello was one of those who drew the water out of the sea at the order of Francis and tasted it before it was blessed, finding it salt ; and then again after it was blessed, when it was sweet.

There were a great many other witnesses who had heard the story from eye-witnesses perfectly worthy of credit, but these two seem to have been the only survivors within reach, of the persons actually present.

The voyage from Singapore to San-Chan —the last voyage of Francis Xavier—was made memorable by several prodigies, and we find incidents of this kind crowded into the few last months of his life, as if he was to be magnified before men, after having incurred so severe a disappointment at Malacca.

After leaving Singapore the vessel was becalmed for fourteen days. They were in all 500 souls on board, and the fresh water was soon consumed. No land was to be seen. The ship lay motionless on the sea, the torrid summer's sun streaming fiercely down upon it from a cloudless sky. Boats were sent out to search for some island that was thought to be not far off, but, after they had ventured as far as they could go with safety, they returned without any result.

In this terrible strait the captain and crew —they were in great part Don Alvaro's people, and so hostile to Francis—remembered that they had the " Great man of God " on board, the power of whose charity and miracles had rung through the whole East. They went to Francis and besought him to help them in their need. Francis placed a cross before them, and bade them all kneel with him and sing a hymn.

Then he retired for a short time into his own cabin to pray, after which he came forth and bade them be of good courage. He had a boat lowered and went into it with a child. He told the child to take some of the sea water and taste it. It was salt. Then he bade him try again. This time it was sweet. On this, Francis went on deck, and ordered the crew to fill all the barrels and vessels they had with the sea water. They obeyed him, but when they tasted the water it was still salt. Then Francis Xavier blessed the water in all the vessels with the sign of the cross, and it was found to be sweeter and fresher than the water of Bangan, as the sailors said.

Bangan was the name of a spring at Goa, the water of which was highly prized. There was enough water, after abundantly supplying all present needs, for the people on board to keep some of it as a treasure, and in this way it became famous over the East, being often used for cures and the like, as if it were the water of some miraculous well.

Boy returned after falling overboard

The calm ceased, and the Santa Croce was able to pursue her course to San-Chan. The remainder of the voyage was full of wonders, which, as we have said, seem crowded to an unusual degree into these, last weeks of the life of Francis.

A Muslim man lost his child, a boy of five years old, who fell overboard at a time when the ship was running fast before the wind, and when it was impossible even to make an attempt to save him. The poor father was in despair for three days, till he chanced to come across Francis Xavier on the deck. It seems that Francis had not heard of the accident. He asked the father whether he would believe in Jesus Christ if his child were restored to him. The man declared he would, and after a few hours he met his child, bright and joyous as ever, running to him on the deck. He kept his promise, and was baptised with all his family.

Most of the testimonies are taken from -"Life of St. Francis Xavier", by H J Coleridge 1874) cross referenced to other works including - Faria Y Sousa The Annals of Portuguese Asia (1655). & Mysteries Marvels Miracles by Joan Carroll Cruz published by Tan Books 1997.

THE FINAL JOURNEY AND DEATH OF A SAINT

In July 1552, after ministering in Indonesia, Malacca, and Japan and who really knows where, Francis felt the pull to China. When he left Goa in 1549 and now in Malacca, Francis had made it clear that he would not see the Christian brothers and sisters again in this life.

The response was much like the sorrow that was expressed when the Apostle Paul left various places for the last time in the book of Acts. Not only had Francis led many of them to Jesus, but he had demonstrated through word and deed the ways of the Kingdom of God. They were loosing their Father in the faith.

Francis was now about to embark on his final journey aboard the Portuguese vessel Santa Croce. The Santa Croce left Malacca and sailed for Singapore, where she stayed for two or three days. We know this because Francis wrote letters to be sent back to Goa and Europe which were dated over these three days. The voyage from Singapore to San Chan, the last in this life that Francis was to make, was a memorable one, filled with many trials and adventures.

Francis writes from Malacca in July 1552; in the planning stages of the journey, "I have written this letter in the midst of many anxieties relating to my passage from this Island to the Chinese continent, it is full of a thousand dangers how it will turn out I know not, but I have a firm assurance in my masters providence and my life is totally in His hands." He continues; "of one thing I am certain, the Devil has a dread of the gospel reaching the ears of the Chinese and The Lord wills me to proclaim it in their hearing".

Just weeks after this letter was written Francis was struck with a fever. It was a Sunday, and the vessel had now been at sea several days. Arriving at San Chan Island Francis was in a bad way. Provisions were running low and it was decided that they would drop Francis and one other off on the Island and seek further provision. This would be the last time that Captain Alvaro Ferreira would ever see Francis alive.

It seems that Francis had long known that His day of departure from this world was at hand, because when he said goodbye to the crew it was with the excitement that he was very soon about to meet with Jesus in his eternal home. The fever gained quick control over Francis who was, rather than being upset, full of hope and joy in the nearness of death. On the Tuesday morning he was lying in the open unable to move but holding a little cross in his hand and was becoming delirious. His servant Antonio attended to his needs. On Friday the 2nd December 1552; at about two in the afternoon, Francis awoke from his fever. He fixed his eyes lovingly on the cross in his hand, his face lit up with joy and tears flooded down his face. He breathed his last after saying,

"Jesus, Master into your hands I commend my Spirit."

His body remained unburied until Sunday morning. It was then that the ship returned to find Francis had passed on to glory. Captain Alvaro had a coffin made for Francis and in order to help the process of decay heaped lime under and over the body of the great man. The understanding was that they would bury Francis in a shallow grave and return at a latter date to transport his remains back to Goa. They planted a wooden cross to mark his grave and amid many tears said farewell to the great man.

In just ten short years Francis had witnessed thousands come to Christ. In his ministry there were 28 people recorded as raised from the dead. Thousands had been healed and set free from all manner of disease. Francis had taught all he converted to pray for the sick and to raise the dead.

This was his mantle and he shared it willingly. Many strange events happened in the life of Francis, some unexplained until this day. One thing is clear Francis was totally dedicated to Jesus, a true mystic and a real saint of his time.

The death of Francis however was not the end of the story and in the next chapter we will explore some of the miracle surrounding his body and the miracles that still occur to this day in Goa when his remains are wheeled throughout he streets of Valah Goa once every ten years.

MIRACLES EVEN IN DEATH

Frances Xavier is one of a number of people known as 'Incorruptible'. These people's bodies don't decay after death but remain fresh, sometimes for hundreds of years. As well as Francis these incorruptibles include; Catherine of Siena, (d1380) Teresa of Avila (d1582) Paschal Baylon(d1592) and many others.

In Francis Xavier's case his body is still not decomposed. Its true I have seen the body myself in the Church of Bon Jesus in Goa India. After over 450 years you can still see it's him, it's a bit dried out now but for over 250 years if you cut the body it still bled.

Here is a quote from the book Mysteries, Marvels & Miracles by Joan Carroll Cruz.

142 years after his death (1694) the body of Francis was given another medical examination. The medical report states the following.

The hair of the saint is black and slightly curly, the forehead is broad and high, showing two rather large veins soft and purple running down the middle. The eyes are dark brown and the gaze is so penetrating that they seem alive. The lips are bright reddish colour and the beard is thick and black. In short this body has all the appearance of still being alive. The tongue is flexible and moist. The blood is fluid, the lips flexible, the flesh soft and in excellent order.

The body is found clean and sound. It is a great marvel and medically impossible, but I cannot deny what I see. I performed this examination in the presence of Mynheer Vandryers the commissioner of the Dutch East Indies Company.

End of quote.

Mynheer Vandryers was so moved by this experience that he repented and became a Christian.

Newsweek magazine in its December 30 1974 issue describes the body as being surprisingly well preserved and very recognisable as someone not long dead. Not bad for someone dead 422 years at the time.

I could speculate as to why these bodies don't decay but that's all it would be "Speculation". The ones who haven't decayed have one thing in common, they were all often caught up in ecstatic encounters with the Lord and often having heavenly visitations. The purpose of this chapter is not to talk about these incorruptible's at length.

Rather I want to share the on going miracles that seem to happen around Francis. There is a biblical precedent of a dead person still carrying the anointing to heal, involving Elisha when they cast the body of a mortally wounded man into Elisha's tomb the man was instantly healed and resurrected.

The following is the account of the discovery of the incorruptible nature of Francis's body.

As discussed in the previous chapter when Francis died he was buried in a shallow grave on the Island of San Chan in the China Sea area on the 2nd Dec 1552 the crew decided to cover him with lime to aid the decay process (this is a practise used at the time so that the flesh would decay quickly and the bones could be transported clean at a latter date) The plan was that they would transport the remains of Francis back to Malacca at a latter time.

In the Life and letters of Francis Xavier it describes the return to the grave at the end of Feb 1553. When the coffin was opened, and the lime removed, the body was found entire, fresh, the flesh soft and succulent the veins full of blood. The Portuguese who made the examination tried to cut a small piece of flesh off from near his knee and blood flowed freely.

The men of the crew some who had been very indifferent to Francis while alive gathered around in wonder many began to weep openly repenting before God. The body was taken as it was in the open coffin and placed on the deck of the Santa Croce in the tropical heat. The captains reasoning was that at least in the heat and humidity the body should begin to break down before they arrived in Malacca. They duly arrived in Malacca on the 22nd March 1553 in the late evening. News of the miracle travelled fast through the town. Medical staff were called to examine the body now deceased for over four months. The report testifies of the wonderful preservation and declares it a miracle.

The next day Francis was carried to Del Monte Church and a great crowd gathered. Even the pagans and Muslims alike recognised the miracle.

The second miracle that day recorded in Portuguese history was that the plague which had been rampant in Malacca for several months completely cleared up on the day Francis arrived back.

They took the body of Francis Xavier and buried it inside the Church. They took it out of its coffin and buried him in the earth. He remained in this grave until August when he was again exhumed because one of the missionaries could not bear to leave Malacca with out seeing the body of Francis one more time.

Diego Pereira and some other friends disinterred the body. Again it was found perfect and fresh as before emitting the most exquisite fragrance. Diego Pereira decided to have the most magnificent coffin made in which the body was laid, until it could be shipped back to Goa where they wanted him to be laid to rest.

So it was that in December 1553 one whole year after his death and still in perfect condition that they set out on board a ship for India.

In January 1554 they arrived in the port of Cochin to be carried north to Goa a short time later. While his body was in Cochin a lady who had been sick and near death heard that the body was returning and had asked to be taken to see it, believing that if she could just see the body she would be made well.

She was carried on board the ship and upon seeing Francis's body in perfect condition was instantly healed. The weather stalled the transfer to Goa but finally on the 15th March 1554 Francis arrived back in Goa.

There was a massive procession through the streets, one eye witness says that tears and open sobbing was almost universal and the sight of the body had people repenting in the streets crying out to Jesus for forgiveness. So for the next 450 years the body has lain in state for all to see. Because of people trying to cut bits off over the years it was put in a huge sealed glass resting place around 1790 and remains there to this day.

I visited the Church of Bon Jesus in 2005 and saw the body with my own eyes. A group of Hindu teenagers from the North were at the Church on a school trip that day and several were overcome by the anointing in the room and sat on the floor sobbing. I was able to speak to them about Jesus and they responded. His body is just a body I know that, but it is the remains of a mighty man of faith.

I can testify that the presence of God in that room is very tangible and many are over come by the feeling of love and mercy coming straight out of heaven. You could say that the presence of God stands guard over the remains. Once every ten years they take his body out and wheel him around the grounds of the cathedral. Every time they do this countless people are healed of incurable diseases.

I can't explain this I just know it's true because I've felt the presence of God there for myself.

Francis would not want us to venerate him but to give all the glory to Jesus, that was who he was. A man passionately following his master no matter what the cost. In life and in death Francis is one of the great missionaries of all time; since the days of the early Apostles at least.

LEANRING FROM THE LIFE OF FRANCIS XAVIER

One of the keys to the amazing ministry of Francis Xavier was his prayer life and devotion to the Lord. On an almost daily basis he went into what the Church at the time called ecstatic encounters. There are many recorded instances where Francis was so deep in intimacy with the Lord he would be caught in a trance. During these trances Francis had many visitations and he also spoke of seeing things in heaven before they happened on earth. Francis had learnt that he was seated with Christ in Heavenly places.

As we then come into the fullness of being seated with Christ the view from heaven changes our mindsets and is a trigger for the miraculous and revival in our hearts and those we speak to.

Eph 2:6 says; For he raised us from the dead along with Christ, and we are seated with him in the heavenly realms—all because we are one with Christ Jesus.

We are the carriers of His glory because of the presence of God in our lives. Francis carried this glory into the high ways and byways of Asia and turned many nations upside down for Jesus.

In John14:19-20, Jesus is recorded as saying. "In just a little while the world will not see me again, but you will. For I will live again, and you will, too. When I am raised to life again, you will know that I am in my Father, and you are in me, and I am in you".

His life was laid down that we might gain access to the portals of heaven, that glory might reign again in the creation of God. His blood brings release from sin & shame to bring the fullness of all that God has and had for his creation. The blood of Jesus removes our sins as far as the east is from the west so that we might boldly enter into the very throne of God. This is where Francis Xavier learned to live and it was to this place that he came on a daily basis.

Hebrews 4:16; encourages us to come boldly to the throne of our gracious God. There we are told we will receive his mercy, and we will find grace to help us when we need it.

And again in Eph 3:12; Because of Christ and our faith in him, we can now come fearlessly into God's presence, assured of his glad welcome.

As His people we have chosen to sit, not in heavenly places but in the dust of worldly thinking. If anyone could have got down about his surroundings and circumstances it would have been Francis Xavier, but in ecstatic bliss he rose into the heavens and into the heart of Jesus.

We are called to enter into the presence of God; not just to experience a tingly feeling down our spine as he passes by, or goose bumps as we catch a glimpse of Him through the veil. But we are called to enter into the realm of the Spirit and to see from a heavenly perspective.

Francis when he spoke, did so out of the atmosphere of heaven. When he prayed for the sick or raised the dead, he prayed out of heaven, not from the earthly perspective but from what he had seen in his encounters. When he worshiped he worshiped in Spirit, sometimes he was lifted to the ceiling in his ecstatic encounter. This is the lesson for us; our whole lives are meant to be a reflection of where we are seated and our worship from out of our encounters.

The Lord showed Francis how to preach the gospel. He saw himself as an ambassador of heaven. Likewise we are called to see ourselves standing on the threshold of heaven With Christ in his glory, and from there speak the atmosphere of heaven into the earthly realm. When heaven invades earth as it does through our link with Christ, then transformation comes.

Our words change, the power we see released changes, Glory is manifest on earth through signs and wonders and unusual miracles in the same way it was through the life of Francis Xavier, because we are speaking out of heaven and not from the position of those who are earthly bound.

Jesus walked in this way and remember, Jesus said, "These things shall you do, and greater than these because I go to my Father" (John14:12)

Jesus was operating from a heavenly perspective all the time; for instance when he called Nathaniel; (John 2:47-51) Jesus said "I saw you under a fig tree." He was seeing Nathaniel and his heart not as men see from an earthly perspective, but from a heavenly perspective. The same with the story of Lazarus (John11); Jesus wasn't hurried or fazed by the circumstance, because he was seeing the event from heaven's perspective. In verse 40 he says "Did I not say to you that if you would believe you would see the glory of God?"

All the miracles he saw from heaven's perspective, and when he spoke He only spoke what He heard from heaven.

You see when we see from heavenly places, time is irrelevant because we are seeing from the eternal realm. You have the ability to see things as they are called to be in the eternal, to see as God sees! And the miraculous is just a release of heaven's glory into this realm.

Isa 48:3 "I have declared the former things from the beginning; they went forth from my mouth, and I caused them to hear it. Suddenly I did them, and they came to pass."

By faith we need to see ourselves in heavenly places, and when you do you will be there. You will hear what the father says, you will see the end and the beginning of an issue and your prayer life will change forever.

Creative miracles, financial miracles, restorative miracles are all waiting in the eternal realm, waiting for us to enter into that realm and see them as God sees them.

To speak them out as we stand in the heavenly portal, to release the glory of God from our position with Christ in heaven. It truly is heaven coming down and transforming the natural realm.

Hebrews 11:1 Faith means being sure of the things we hope for and knowing that something is real even if we do not see it.

We can only understand what's happening around us if, by faith we enter the realms of glory, we can only understand the earthly realm if we view it from a higher realm. We cannot understand the fallen world by viewing it through fallen eyes, we have to go to a higher vantage point, to the place where Jesus is, and where we are called to dwell. The natural realm is given to the sons of men, but we who are in Christ are the sons of God (John 1:12). We are called to live in another realm, the realm of glory, so we have to learn to operate from where we come from. We are Eagles not turkeys. heavenly beings, not earth bound.

The plan of the enemy is to keep the people of God earth bound through religious mindsets and arguments. It so saddens me to hear people say that they don't want to enter into the realms of the Spirit, into that place of standing in heaven with Jesus, of seeing the earth from the perspective of heaven, because they are afraid of the spiritual. If you are in Christ, then your home is in the supernatural realm of heaven with Christ. You are in the world, but not of the world.

The reformation in 1514 was essentially a German one and there wasn't any room for the mystical side of the Catholic Church that the likes of Francis Xavier and Ignatius Loyola exhibited in their lives.

Every move of God releases revelation, why? Because heaven invades the mindsets of the people of God, and they see from the position of glory where we are all called to be seated. Why does revival tarry? It's simple really; our mind sets have not been invaded by heaven, we are too earth bound! This contradicts the statement made by many earth bound saints that says "Oh he's too heavenly minded to be of any earthly good." Every breakthrough in science, every literary breakthrough, every social breakthrough has come as people see from a heavenly perspective.

Both Xavier and Loyola were put in prison at times because they were considered too extreme in their ecstatic love for Jesus. Who can remember the names of those who put them in prison and what did they achieve?

The healing revival in the 1940's saw the miracles of God released. The Charismatic move saw grace and lay ministry accepted; Toronto saw the Fathers heart revealed. Every new wave of Glory brings with it fresh Manna from heaven. Don't limit God or put Him in a doctrinal box but seek to stand with Christ in heavenly places and live in that place like Francis.

One thing all moves of God have in common is that they were all opposed by those who had a religious mindset. When your vision exceeds what others are seeing from an earthly perspective, religion says "it's not of God." But history tells us that Francis Xavier saw from a heavenly perspective and mindsets were changed and the known world turned upside down.

My desire is to see heaven released in this

way in many Church groups, an activation of the heavenly realm. All we are called to do is act as ushers to the purpose of God and speak out of the portals of heaven.

You can change your world today as you choose to rise into heavenly places and let the Glory invade your thinking. God is raising up a people to tear down mindsets. The mindsets that would have contained Francis Xavier in the courts of the King of Portugal are still active today.

Francis saw his call from heaven's perspective and gave up all to follow the vision. The challenge for us today is, are we trying to contain God in our earthly box, or are we going to see ourselves seated with Christ? Are we going to scoff at the seers & prophets who begin to call us into heavenly places or are we going to rise up with Christ? As the Apostles begin to call us into a heavenly mindset, are we going to dig our toes in and remain earth bound or are we going to walk into our heavenly inheritance?

God is doing something fresh in your spirit. You can feel the life surge through you as you read this. It's time to shake off your old mindsets, and cross the line into heavenly places, to breath in the atmosphere of Heaven which is Glory and then standing in it, proclaim what you see into this realm. If you desire transformation in your Church or ministry, then you need to see that there is no other way to achieve your dreams; only as you live in the glory will your dreams become a reality.

Eph 2:6; For he raised us from the dead along with Christ, and we are seated with him in the heavenly realms—all because we are one with Christ Jesus.

The life of Francis Xavier still speaks. He calls us up into the heavens and it is here that we must dwell all the days of our life.

FRANCIS XAVIER'S LIFE STILL CHANGES US

Francis Xavier is an inspiration to all who aspire to reach the lost. The secret to his supernatural ministry was an abandoned heart to the purpose of God. In most of his ministry he emulated his master in that he spent hours in prayer before the Father, and only moved or acted when he had instructions to do so.

Francis was saved at the age of 18 or 19 and from that time was abandoned to Jesus, but the ministry years, a 10 year window between 1541 & 1552 were very intense. The mission of Francis Xavier was effective in reaching the un-reached because it came with demonstrations of God's Glory, power, miracles, signs and wonders. Francis would be the first to say that the supernatural gifts he moved in were not from him, but from the Master whom he loved and abandoned his life to.

The supernatural manifestations of the Holy Spirit are the foundation stones upon which the church was established and upon which it stands. The miracles in Francis Xavier's life came out of relationship with Jesus and abandoned obedience to the purpose of God. Miracles and supernatural manifestations seen in the Life of Francis are meant to be the normal experiences of every believer in the supernaturally founded, supernaturally filled, and supernaturally directed church of Jesus Christ.

As we have seen Francis was very human and prone to depressions and despair. His strength and passion was found in his relationship with Jesus.

This relationship produced a zeal and passion that led him in an ecstasy of love for Jesus. It seems at times his heart would burst with the joy of knowing him. As he filled his soul again and again in these times of set apartness, the stage was set for the next season of miracles, preaching to the lost and serving the poor and sick wherever he found himself.

Francis Xavier was an ordinary human being, in a love relationship with an extraordinary God. His life serves as a reminder to us that if we ask Jesus to show us his will for our lives, and then only do what we hear the Holy Spirit tell us to do, We, as ordinary human vessels can turn our world upside down. Don't let the times of discouragement rob you of the whole purpose of God, but set yourselves apart to hear what the Father is saying and do it.

Remember every miracle that happens supernaturally in our life is released out of relationship with the Holy Spirit. No matter how insignificant you see yourself in God's Kingdom, all can make a difference because it's not about us, it's about Him.

Francis Xavier had prayed for Martyrdom all his Christian life but he didn't die a martyr. Instead he died on the damp, cold ground of San Chan Island with an uncontrollable fever. He wasn't very old when he died; born in 1506 he died on December 2nd 1552 only 46 years old. Yet in those 46 years he turned the world upside down for Jesus.

The life of Francis Xavier still speaks to us, inspiring us to a fresh wave of supernatural missions and mystical life in Christ. In an era when many have said that sending missionaries doesn't work any longer we need to reflect on the life of this man Francis Xavier and realise that nothing has changed, people are still hungry for a demonstration of who God is. In the immediate past missions have concentrated on education, health, welfare, digging wells and feeding the poor all these are wonderful and to be commended but none of these endeavours changed geographical regions like Francis did.

In our current age I can think of two missionary families who are practicing this method of mission. Heidi & Rolland Baker in Mozambique and the Hogan family in México. Both missions are gaining thousands of souls for Christ.

If we serve a supernatural God who lives in a supernatural place and demonstrates supernatural attributes should we not also be living in a supernatural demonstration of the mission of Christ?

The life of Francis is also a reflection of supernatural Kingdom provision having the full backing of the royal family of Portugal. We can't expect this sort of backing without being prepared to lay down our lives like Francis. His all for the Kingdom lifestyle touched hearts all the way to the King of a nation. He didn't just talk about mission he lived the mission of Christ. Demonstrating resurrection power, he lived totally in the realm of dreams, visions and mystical trances.

He marched against entire armies and won; but most of all he was in ecstatic union with Christ. To Francis nothing else mattered, the religious system around him acted as a framework for his ministry, but he was never confined to its narrowness, instead he saw heaven and acted it out on earth.

The challenge of this little book is to ask the question, "where is the next Francis Xavier?" Perhaps it is you as you have read these pages.

A Prayer for Missions
By Francis Xavier.

O eternal God, creator of all things, remember that the souls of the lost have been created by you out of nothing, and formed after your own image and likeness. Behold Lord, to the dishonour of your name, Hell is peopled with them. Remember that Jesus your Son suffered for their salvation the most cruel death; Permit not, I beseech you, O Lord that your Son be any longer held in contempt by the lost. But appeased by the prayers of your Church the most Holy Spouse of your Son, remember your mercy, forget their infidelity. Grant that they might be saved through your Son Jesus, whom you have sent and in whom is our salvation, our life and our liberty to whom be all Glory for ever and Ever. Amen.

Bibliography.

1) A collection of the letters of Francis Xavier by Father Menchacha & M. Leon Pages (1850) Out of print

2) Faria Y Sousa The Annals of Portuguese Asia (1655) Out of print.

3) Mysteries Marvels Miracles by Joan Carroll Cruz published by Tan Books 1997

4) I am mostly indebted to the work of **Henry James Coleridge** The life and letters of Francis Xavier, Burns & Oats publisher London. (1874) out of print.

5) The Basilica of Bon Jesus in Valha Goa, India which contains the mortal remains of Francis Xavier and its display museum has also offered information and inspiration.

6) For the Greater Glory of God – A spiritual retreat with Ignatius Loyola by Manuel Ruiz Jurado – Published by The word among us Press, USA.

7) Francis Xavier – by Aloysius Lazarus – Published by Pauline Publications Bombay India.

8) New Living Translation of the Bible – Tyndale House Publishers.

9) Saints who raised the Dead- over 400 resurrection Miracles – by Father Albert J Hebert – Published by Tan Books 1986

There is every reason to accept that the Portuguese history of Francis Xavier is very accurate and trustworthy. All the acts and miracles are supported by sworn witnesses on order of the King of Portugal. The depositions are as carefully drawn as any that pass current legal investigations and would stand up in a modern court of law.

MAN ON A MISSION

Francis Xavier is a name you often see on Schools, Hospitals and Universities but who is Francis Xavier and what impact could someone who lived nearly 500 years ago have on my life today? Possibly having the greatest missionary impact since the Apostle Paul, Francis Xavier's life challenges us today. A man who knew Jesus and chose to lay down his life in order to serve him, Francis saw thousands come to faith in Jesus and his life was full of supernatural encounters with the Living God. 28 people are historically & verifiably recorded as being raised from the dead through Francis Xavier's ministry (there were possibly hundreds.) Countless thousands were healed and set free Whole nations were impacted in a ten year window of time 1542-1552. This book will challenge and inspire you and who knows you may be the next Francis Xavier in your generation.

Ian Johnson is the Author of Man on a mission and as a result of visiting Xavier's final resting place in Goa India in 2005 has had a burden to see powerful and supernatural missions released in the earth again.

Francis Xavier was an ordinary human being who had on-going encounters with an extraordinary God. The key to Francis Xavier's ministry was ecstatic encounters and a belief that God will go to any lengths to see the Kingdom of Jesus established on earth. Francis Xavier went and demonstrated the glory of the gospel with signs following, and King John 111 of Portugal sent him out funding his projects across the East wherever the Portuguese settled. This was the perfect Mission, one who went and one who sent. The result, was Kingdom glory.

MP3 Messages by Ian Johnson

MP3 Messages from the ministry of Ian Johnson
are available for downloading from

Set Time Media
www.settimemedia.com

**To book Ian Johnson for Church or
Conference speaking engagements
contact the ministry by e-mail
ianjohn@xtra.co.nz**

**View our Web-site
www.hisamazinggloryministries.org**

or

His Amazing Glory Facebook page.

OTHER TITLES
BY
IAN JOHNSON

Glory to Glory
A Journey of Intimacy & Worship

Into the heart of Jesus
A 21 day journey into an Intimate walk

Anzac's Israel & God
The ANZAC legacy & modern Israel

Gems from Heaven
A collection of quotes from the ministry of Ian Johnson

All titles Available From

His Amazing Glory Ministries
4 Ewing Road RD4 Tuakau
2694, New Zealand.

Ph (09)2368126
E-mail ianjohn@xtra.co.nz

ABOUT THE AURTHOR

Saved in 1977 as a result of a face to face encounter with Jesus; Ian Johnson has always sought to live in a life of encounter and intimacy with the Lord. With a heart for history, Ian has discovered that in every century the Church has demonstrated the supernatural. He has made it his mission to communicate the mystical and supernatural realm of the Kingdom of God to this current generation.

Ian Has been in ministry for over 25 years having pioneered and led Churches in the South Auckland area of New Zealand.

Ian and Joye Johnson travel as itinerant ministers speaking in Churches and conferences in NZ, Australia and the nations. Currently Ian is on the leadership team at Horizon Church in Auckland, New Zealand.

His Amazing Glory Ministries

Ian & Joye Johnson travel the nation & the nations opening realms of glory. Based at Horizon Church in Auckland New Zealand where they are part of the governmental leadership team. Ian speaks at Church and conference's as a sought after prophetic ministry.

To book Ian Johnson for Church or Conference speaking engagements contact the ministry by e-mail ianjohn@xtra.co.nz

www.ingramcontent.com/pod-product-compliance
Lightning Source LLC
Chambersburg PA
CBHW060416050426
42449CB00009B/1983